My Best Frier

GW01459901

Written by
Kathleen Prior & Roisin Hickey
Illustrated by Roisin Hickey

Chosen Children's Books
N. Ireland

For
Kevin, Mairead, Fiona,
Sean, Kerry, Clare, Mark,
Michael, Catherine, Christine,
Lauren, Louise and all Jesus' special helpers.

Published by Chosen Children's Books, N. Ireland.

ISBN 0-9528739-1-5

Printed in Singapore.

God our Father
looked down from heaven above
and said, "The time has come
to send the world pure love.
When My precious Son is born upon the earth,
My greatest gift of love will come to birth."

3

In a stable Jesus our brother was born.
An ox and a donkey kept Him warm.
Our Father smiled from heaven above
and said, "I send My Son with love."

A shepherd boy came with his sheep.
He peeped at Jesus fast asleep.
Wise men came with gifts for the little King.
Heavenly angels began to sing,
"Glory be to God above,
and peace on earth to all who love."

Bless You, Jesus, for being born.
Bless You, Jesus, for Christmas morn.
Jesus, my brother, You're my very best friend.

Baby Jesus was taken to the temple one day
to be presented to God in a prayerful way.
Our Father smiled from heaven above
and said, "I bless My Son with love."

When Anna and Simeon saw little baby Jesus,
He was eight days old, so tiny and precious.
"At last He is here! Here is the Messiah
whom we've waited to see with a burning desire!
Now we can go to heaven and rest."
Anna and Simeon felt truly blessed.

Bless You, Jesus, for babies so precious.
Bless You, Jesus, for coming to save us.
Jesus, my brother, You're my very best friend.

Mary and Joseph searched the big city,
for Jesus was lost. Oh, what a pity!
Our Father smiled from heaven above
and said, "Seek My Son with love."

After three days, Mary and Joseph came
to the temple in Jerusalem.
With the teachers sat their twelve-year-old boy,
speaking of His heavenly Father with great joy.
He said, "You didn't have to search for Me.
I'm in My Father's house, you see."

Bless You, Jesus, for parents who care.
Bless You, Jesus, for families that share.
Jesus, my brother, You're my very best friend.

To a wedding feast in Cana, Jesus went to dine.
He worked His first miracle when
He changed water into wine.
Our Father smiled from heaven above
and said, "Ask My Son with love."

Mary spoke to her precious Son,
"The party is not over but the wine is done."
Mary told the servants to do as Jesus willed.
He said, "See that the wine jugs with water are filled."
When the guests drank to quench their thirst,
they asked why the best wine had not been served first.

Bless You, Jesus, for hearing my prayer.
Bless You, Jesus, for miracles everywhere.
Jesus, my brother, You're my very best friend.

When Jesus set out to teach
the Good News,
He chose twelve apostles
from among His fellow Jews.
Our Father smiled from heaven above
and said, "Follow My Son with love."

"Peter, Andrew, James and John
follow Me. Please come along."
Jesus then called eight more men
to join this special band of friends.
They would learn He was God's Son—
the Messiah they were waiting on.

Bless You, Jesus. You call me too.
Bless You, Jesus. I'll follow You.
Jesus, my brother, You're my very best friend.

15

For three years Jesus
went throughout Galilee,
spreading love and working
miracles for everyone to see.
Our Father smiled from heaven above
and said, "Believe in My Son with love."

When they needed help the people came,
and Jesus cured their blind and lame.
He took away the sinners' pain,
telling them, "Go, love again."
People followed Him from place to place,
for they saw this man was full of grace.

Bless You, Jesus. Your love and mercy flow.
Bless You, Jesus. Your grace helps me to grow.
Jesus, my brother, You're my very best friend.

On Holy Thursday, while sharing a meal, Jesus stood
and changed bread and wine into spiritual food.
Our Father smiled from heaven above
and said, "Share this food of love."

Jesus' friends begged Him to stay
when He told them He was going away.
So He changed bread and wine into spiritual food
to make them strong and keep them good.
"Do this in My memory, friends,
and I'll always be with you. My love has no end."

Bless You, Jesus. Your love brings us together.
Bless You, Jesus. Stay with me forever.
Jesus, my brother, You're my very best friend.

Jealous men hung Jesus on the Cross to die.
His faithful friends started to cry.
Our Father smiled from heaven above
and said, "My Son dies for love."

On Good Friday, for love, Jesus died.
To save us, He was crucified.
His friends were full of sorrow,
for they missed their loving brother;
but they were not sad for long,
for Jesus kept His promise to return.

Bless You, Jesus. It was for me You died.
Bless the wounds in Your hands, feet and side.
Jesus, my brother, You're my very best friend.

23

On Easter Sunday Jesus came to life again,
and showed Himself to special friends.
Our Father smiled from heaven above
and said, "My Son lives and loves."

Though soldiers guarded Jesus in the tomb,
He rolled away the stone and left that rocky room.
Two women visiting His resting-place,
were greeted by an angel's smiling face.
"Jesus is risen! He is alive!
Go spread the Good News of this awesome surprise."

Bless You, Jesus, for Easter Sunday;
for chocolate eggs and the Easter bunny.
Jesus, my brother, You're my very best friend.

On Ascension Day, before His friends' eyes,
Jesus returned to paradise.
Our Father smiled from heaven above
and said, "My Son leaves you His love."

Jesus went home after forty days.
A glorious sight! His friends stood amazed.
They thought of His promise, "We'll never part, for
My Father will send the Holy Spirit to live in your hearts.
Then you will tell each precious little child
about Jesus, their best friend and loving guide."

Bless You, Jesus, for new life everywhere.
May I tend this gift with loving care.
Jesus, my brother, You're my very best friend.

Love

Every morning when I wake up, Jesus I say, "Hi!"
and invite You to come in and stay close by.
I say, "Please help me show Your love today
to everyone I meet at work and play.
I know You're always with me,
when I'm happy, when I'm sad.
Jesus, You're the best friend I ever had."